TOUGH QUESTIONS

RAY COMFORT // EMEAL ("E.Z.") ZWAYNE // MARK SPENCE

Apologetics Made Simple

STUDY GUIDE

Living Waters Publications
Bellflower, CA

Tough Questions: Apologetics Made Simple
Study Guide

Published by
Living Waters Publications
P.O. Box 1172
Bellflower, CA 90707, USA
LivingWaters.com

ISBN 978-1-936906-40-6

Edited by Lynn Copeland

Design and production by Genesis Group

Printed in the United States of America

Unless otherwise indicated, Scripture quotations are from the *New King James* version, © 1979, 1980, 1982 by Thomas Nelson Inc., Publishers, Nashville, Tennessee.

"But sanctify the Lord God in your hearts,
and **ALWAYS BE READY**
to give a defense to everyone who asks you
a reason for the hope that is in you,
with meekness and fear."

1 PETER 3:15

CONTENTS

GETTING STARTED

Welcome to the "Tough Questions" apologetics study. We commend you for being a faithful fisher of men (and women) and for desiring to become better equipped in your evangelistic efforts. Apologetics is an intimidating topic to many, but this study will help you discover that even tough questions can be answered simply and conversationally, in a way that guides your listeners to consider the claims of the gospel.

Whether you are encountering questions from friends and family, or you want to be prepared to give answers as you speak with strangers, we trust this course will increase your confidence and provide handy tools for your arsenal while you reach the lost.

Although this course can be used for individual study, it is ideally suited for use in small and large groups. A group setting can provide the needed encouragement and accountability.

For group use, notes for the leader are highlighted in the lessons. Be sure to review these in planning the study and preordering materials. This kit includes one Study Guide and enough tracts to get you started, but be sure to order additional Study Guides so that each participant has their own and sufficient tracts to complete the homework assignments.

HOW TO USE THIS STUDY

Each session includes the following parts:

- **Open in Prayer:** Begin each lesson in prayer, asking God to give you a deeper understanding of His Word and a genuine concern for the lost.

- **Share Your Experiences:** As you put into practice what you're learning each week, and begin sharing these biblical truths with the lost, hearing one another's experiences will build your confidence. Be sure to allow adequate time for this interaction.

- **Ray / For Your Reflection:** Read this thought-provoking text before viewing the video, to prepare your heart for the class.

- **View the Video:** Watch the video as a group. The video sessions are approximately 30 minutes in length.

- **Discussion Questions:** As time allows, discuss these questions to help you recall the information learned in the video and apply it to your life. Depending on your group size, you may want to divide into smaller groups to discuss the questions. Allow each participant to express his thoughts, being careful to avoid arguing or having anyone dominate the conversation.

- **Quote // Unquote:** These words of wisdom, from notable apologists, add insights on the important role of apologetics.

- **A Ready Answer:** These additional questions and answers will further equip you to "give a defense [answer] to everyone who asks you" a reason for your hope. These ready answers have been gleaned from *The Evidence Bible* (compiled by Ray Comfort), where you can find hundreds more.

- **Sharing Made Simple:** Apologetics isn't something to build your intellect in an ivory tower, but to share with the real world on the dusty road of life. These weekly practical assignments are the most important part of the study. Every week you will be challenged to gradually stretch your evangelistic muscles, interact with others, and share what you have learned with the lost in your community.

To receive the maximum benefit from this study, please commit to completing these activities. You will be expected to share these experiences with others during the next session.

- **Digging Deeper:** This at-home Bible study will delve deeper into the biblical foundations of the topics covered in the video. God's Word is powerful, and in searching it you will discover wonderful truths that reinforce what you're learning in class.

- **Memory Verse:** Each session includes a Scripture verse to commit to memory. These will help guide your attitudes and actions as you prepare to bring biblical truths to the lost.

Whether you're completing this study in a home group, Sunday school class, or discipleship training class, we pray that you will become well equipped with ready answers as you share the message of everlasting life with a world that desperately needs to hear it.

APOLOGETICS DEFINED

OPEN IN PRAYER

SHARE YOUR EXPERIENCES

Go around the room and, one at a time, briefly share why you have come to this class. What are you hoping to accomplish by taking this course? Are you wanting to have answers to feel more confident to begin witnessing, or to further develop your current evangelism skills? If you're already sharing your faith and have encountered questions that you can't answer, what kinds of questions were they? How did you respond to the situation?

RAY // FOR YOUR REFLECTION

You're at an office party on the tenth floor of a high-rise when you hear the distant sound of sirens. Everyone rushes to the windows to see what's happening. They are looking at another high-rise about eight feet across a narrow alley from your building.

Smoke is billowing from a window and you can see that a number of people are trapped! You hear gasps from those around you as they come to grips with the reality that within minutes, they are going to see people burned alive in front of their eyes. Suddenly of one your coworkers turns and runs out of the office in a seeming panic. You wonder why he would be so cowardly as to run away.

Moments later, he comes crashing through the door like a madman, runs across the office, and smashes the window with the front of a ten-foot ladder. The group rushes to help him to secure the ladder into the window of the opposing building. It is then that you see the wisdom of what he was doing as those trapped people begin, one by one, to crawl across the ladder to safety.

What was it that caused people to crawl across a ladder? It was fear! It was the knowledge of what would happen to them if they stayed in the building.

Now think what this same gesture would have meant to them if they didn't know that their building was on fire and their lives at stake. If they thought that they were safe, someone in another building shoving a ladder into their building would be more than meaningless. It would be alarming harassment, worthy of a call to the police.

In this study we will be looking at apologetics arguments, which should be seen as a means to an end. We are hoping that unbelievers will believe us when we move from arguments to the wonderful claims of the gospel. What we want is to say, "Your building is on fire!" and have them understand their predicament.

Apologetics alone does little to alarm sinners. Our arguments and answers can serve as an attention-getter, but they don't show the lost world their terrible plight. They merely sound a distant alarm. What sinners need is to smell the smoke, feel the heat, and think of their terrifying fate.

The whole sinful world is in a burning building, in danger of being engulfed in flames. But sin is seen as a pleasure rather than a pain. The gospel is foolishness to them (1 Corinthians 1:18), and they see our pleading as nothing but harassment. We talk of everlasting life being a free gift of God, and they accuse us of "pushing religion down their throats." Their rejection of the best news they could ever hope to hear is unbelievable—unbelievable, that is, until you understand what is happening. They love their sin. And what's more, in their view God doesn't seem to be bothered by it, so it's no big deal. Lying, stealing, lust, blasphemy, fornication, and even adultery don't bring any evident divine lightning. And so they remain in their sinful stupor until the Law, in the hand of the Spirit, awakens them. (We will look at that subject in the next session.)

Apologetics, therefore, should always be seen as a means to an end—and the end is salvation through the gospel.

VIEW THE VIDEO // Apologetics Defined (26 minutes)

DISCUSSION QUESTIONS

1. Define the word "apologetics" and give its origin. Should we be apologizing for our faith?

2. Discuss the meaning of 1 Peter 3:15. Does it imply that we should wait for people to ask us about our faith before engaging them in conversation?

3. Name two basic types of apologetics and explain the differences. What are the times we should use each one?

4. What is the foundation of the Christian's authority?

5. Using Romans chapter 1, explain why we can know that everyone believes in the existence of God. Why don't many people acknowledge it?

6. In what way can we focus too much on apologetics?

7. Should we answer every question we are asked? Why or why not?

8. What is your typical response when someone knocks on your door? How does that compare to the way Mark and his family respond, and how can you do something similar?

9. Why shouldn't we ask for permission to start a conversation? (See Matthew 28:19; Mark 16:15.) What can happen if we do?

10. How could you respond if someone says, "There's no such thing as absolute truth"?

QUOTE // UNQUOTE

"The only way [to] become truly 'prepared to give an answer to everyone who asks' (1 Pet. 3:15) is by wrestling personally with the questions. Ironically, those who have never grappled with diverse worldviews are actually the most likely to be swept away by them. As G. K. Chesterton wrote, ideas can be dangerous—but they are far more dangerous to the person who has never studied them… We should always couch discussions of Christianity in the language of reasons and evidence. We should be giving apologetics from the pulpit and in the Sunday school classroom. Every course in a Christian school should be an opportunity to show that a biblical perspective does a better job than any secular theory of accounting for the facts in that field, whether psychology, biology, government, or business. Apologetics should be naturally woven in to all our discourse."

—Nancy Pearcey

A READY ANSWER

Much of what we do in life has its foundation in trust. We trust our dentist when he drills, our taxi driver when he drives, our pilots when they fly us. We trust our history books, our teachers, and some still even trust politicians. Marriage is a trust relationship. So are business partnerships and friendships. We trust elevators, planes, cars, brakes, chairs, doctors, surgeons, brokers, and television anchors. We place our faith in these items and people based on evidence that they are trustworthy. It's therefore hard to understand why skeptics mock the thought of trust in God.

This skeptic's statement implies that Christians are living by a naïve, "blind" faith based on something for which we have no evidence, when the opposite is the case. Our faith is rational and reasonable, and is based on credible, verifiable, historical evidence. The God who created us has given us all the evidence we need to come to know Him, and He invites us, "Come now, and let us reason together" (Isaiah 1:18).

The fact that some do not recognize the evidence doesn't mean it is not there. God has given light to every man (John 1:9)—through this wonderful creation, through the undeniable voice of the conscience, and through plain old common sense. We have the Bible's thousands of fulfilled prophecies, as well as "many infallible proofs" of the resurrection (Acts 1:3), and He even promises to reveal Himself to those who obey Him (John 14:21).

It is also important to explain the difference between believing something (the Bible) and trusting Someone (Jesus Christ). Skeptics think that a Christian is someone who simply "believes" in God's existence. When the Bible speaks of "faith" in God, it is not a reference to an intellectual acknowledgment that He exists (we all intuitively know that). It is speaking of an implicit trust in His person and His promises. There's nothing difficult about having trust or "faith" when the One you are trusting is utterly trustworthy.

(Excerpted from *The Evidence Bible*.)

SHARING MADE SIMPLE

 Group Leader: *Provide enough tracts to give each person ten. Samples were included in the kit; order more as needed.*

Throughout this course, we're going to be taking steps to share the gospel with those who desperately need to hear it—one simple step at a time. This week, your first task is to think about the reality of Hell for two whole minutes. This will take discipline, because your mind will want to wander, especially because these are not pleasant thoughts.

Think of the worst pain you've ever experienced—toothache, a broken arm, a headache that brings you to tears, or perhaps a painful burn that kept you awake all night. Then think of what Hell is going to be like for the unsaved. Put yourself in that terrible place, and think of the utter despair and hopelessness of eternal damnation. That means the pain and anguish will never stop.

The object in doing this unpleasant exercise is to move from a concern to a painful empathy—your own mental anguish as you think of the fate of the lost. If you find yourself in that state of mind, hold onto it as you would precious gold. This is because it will help you to overcome paralyzing fear at the thought of witnessing. It is empathy that causes a courageous firefighter to run into a burning building to save perishing strangers. It goes hand-in-hand with love.

Empathy will help you to love your neighbor as yourself and therefore be concerned for his salvation as much as you're concerned for your own. Don't let it go because you're especially going to need it when you hear of this week's assigned step.

Here it is: Go to your local university, get up on a soapbox and plead with this dying and Hell-bound world. *Just kidding.* I wouldn't ask you to do that. Not just yet. But by thinking for a moment that it was this week's task, it should make it easier for you to hear what the task actually is. It is simply to leave ten gospel tracts where people can find them. Compared to going to your local university, getting up on a box and pleading with sinners, this step is a piece of cake. A very small piece.

As we heard in the video, "If you don't get to the gospel, you've lost the argument—it doesn't matter how eloquent your words are." And gospel tracts are the easiest way to start sharing the message of eternal life. This isn't a marathon you are being asked to run; it's just one simple step of faith. If you don't take your first step, you will never run the race.

DIGGING DEEPER

1. In the following verses, record everything the Bible says about our responsibilities in witnessing (what, when, and how):

Philippians 1:17

1 Peter 3:15

Jude 3

Colossians 4:6

2 Timothy 4:2

2. In the above admonitions, which aspects would you say you most need help with (knowing what to say, or how to say it)?

3. Truth is what corresponds to reality, yet the world today increasingly claims there is no such thing as "truth." In contrast, write what the Bible tells us about the source of truth:

John 1:17

John 14:6

John 17:17

4. Read what Jesus said about truth in John 18:37,38. Why do you think Pilate questioned what truth is? Why would he walk away before hearing the answer? How is this like our society today?

5. First Timothy 2:4 assures us that God desires all men to be saved and to come to the knowledge of the truth. What can we learn from the following verses about why the lost reject the concept of truth?

John 8:44

Galatians 3:1

Romans 1:18,25

2 Timothy 4:3–5

MEMORY VERSE

"Be diligent to present yourself approved to God, a worker who does not need to be ashamed, rightly dividing the word of truth." —**2 Timothy 2:15**

THE NATURE OF THE PROBLEM

OPEN IN PRAYER

SHARE YOUR EXPERIENCES

Briefly share the results of the previous session's "Sharing Made Simple" assignment. You were to leave ten gospel tracts in public where someone could find them. What kinds of places did you leave them? Did you get a sense of joy or accomplishment in doing this?

RAY // FOR YOUR REFLECTION

Before doctors can prescribe a treatment, they must first come to a determination of the likely cause of the disease. They identify the nature of the illness by doing some probing, examining the patient's symptoms, and then make a diagnosis.

We must do the same spiritually. All of humanity is inflicted with the fatal disease of sin, and Christians have been entrusted with the only cure: the gospel of Jesus Christ. There is no point in offering God's grace—the message of mercy, the good news of the cross—to someone who is proud and self-righteous, because the person will simply thumb his nose at it. He won't be interested in the cure when he doesn't know he has a disease.

One effective way to diagnose where someone is spiritually is to probe with a question about the nature of humanity. Does the person you're speaking with think human beings are good or evil? Almost every secular person will respond with something like, "Mankind is basically good, but we have our weaknesses." Very rarely will this world say that someone is "evil" unless he is in the category of Adolf Hitler. This generation is so brainwashed by godless secular humanism that it can't even define good or evil. So name some serious crimes and ask if the person would say these are good or evil: "Murder, rape, pedophilia, torture, adultery, lying, stealing, abortion, fornication—are these things morally wrong?" As you go though the list, watch him make subjective judgments. Whether or not something is good or evil will usually be dependent on his feelings. More than likely, underneath his attempts to justify mankind, he is attempting to justify himself. None of us like to think that we are evil.

The reason good and evil are nebulous to a non-Christian is that, according to his worldview, there is no absolute standard of morality from which he can judge himself. By establishing his own relative standard, each person thinks that he is good (Proverbs 20:6). That's why we need the moral Law—a universal standard that applies to all people in all places at all times. That's the reason we bring the Ten Commandments into the picture when witnessing, as Jesus did. When the rich young ruler ran up and knelt before Him, asking, "Good Teacher, what shall I do that I may inherit eternal life?," Jesus first corrected his understanding of good. He said that only God is good, and then He pointed the man to God's standard of goodness, the Ten Commandments (see Mark 10:17–22). It's the straightness of the moral Law that reveals the crookedness of the human heart.

DISCUSSION QUESTIONS

1. Most questions unbelievers ask come from a misunderstanding of the Fall. Explain what it is and some of the evidences of it, both in ourselves and in our world.

2. What are some ways unbelievers try to pass the blame when it comes to sin? Why are we each accountable to God for our actions?

3. How can we become proficient when it comes to answering questions? Where's a good place to start?

4. Is it okay not to have all the answers? Explain.

5. How could you respond if someone claims God is evil for commanding genocide?

6. Why are skeptics inconsistent when they say it's evil to kill the Canaanites, or that God is immoral?

7. In what ways do the ungodly seek to justify man? (See Job 32:2; 40:8.)

8. What is the Socratic method, and how can we use it?

9. If someone asks why God allows suffering, what are ways you could respond?

10. Why should we precede the gospel with the moral Law? What effect does that have on the skeptic's questions?

QUOTE // UNQUOTE

" As that which is straight discovers that which is crooked, as the looking-glass shows us our natural face with all its spots and deformities, so there is no way of coming to that knowledge of sin which is necessary to repentance, and consequently to peace and pardon, but by comparing our hearts and lives with the Law. "

—Matthew Henry

A READY ANSWER

"Do I really need to 'prove' God to anyone or just preach the gospel?"

We do not have to prove to the atheist that God exists. He intuitively knows that God exists but willfully suppresses the truth (Romans 1:18). Every person has a God-given conscience, which is the "work of the law written in their hearts" (Romans 2:15). Just as every sane person knows that it is wrong to lie, steal, kill, and commit adultery, he knows that if there is a moral Law, then there must be a moral Lawgiver (James 4:12). In addition to the testimony of his impartial conscience, the atheist also has the testimony of creation. It declares the glory of God, His eternal power, and divine nature, so that the person who denies the voice of conscience and the voice of creation is without excuse (Psalm 19:1; Romans 1:19–21). If he dies in his sins, he will face the wrath of a holy Creator, whether he believes in Him or not.

This is why I don't spend too much effort trying to convince anyone that there is a God. To do so is to waste time and energy. What sinners need is not to be convinced that God exists, but that their sin exists and that they are in terrible danger. The only biblical way to do this is to go through the moral Law and explain that God considers lust to be adultery and hatred to be murder (Matthew 5:28; 1 John 3:15), etc. It is the revelation that God is holy and just, and sees the thought-life, that convinces us that we are in danger of eternal damnation. That is what sinners need to hear to send them to the cross for mercy. So never be discouraged from preaching the gospel, and don't get sidetracked by rabbit-trail issues that don't really matter.

(Excerpted from *The Evidence Bible*.)

SHARING MADE SIMPLE

 Group Leader: *Provide enough tracts to give each person ten.*

This week you're going to take your second step toward sharing the reason for our hope with the lost. You took the first step last week when you left ten gospel tracts somewhere in public.

Your assignment for the week is to give out another ten tracts. You can leave most of them somewhere they'll be found—but with at least one, hand it to someone personally. Just say, "Good morning. Did you get one of these?" and then hand out the tract. You can do this. When you get nervous, pull yourself together by thinking of the fate of the stranger before you. Then say to yourself, "This is ridiculous. I'm not going to die if I hand someone a piece of paper! With the help of God, I will give away this tract, if it's the last thing I do." Then do it. You will be glad you did.

If you feel like running the second the person takes hold of it, you're normal. You're like me. I have given away hundreds of thousands of tracts to individuals, and I still feel like running away every time, because they will see that it's about God and will reject me. I'm a wimp. But it gets even worse. If somebody doesn't want it, I become like a spoiled little child. I want to say something unkind to them—because I feel hurt. Knowing that you're not alone with your fears will hopefully be some source of consolation to you.

Keep in mind that if you get rejected, it may not be because you're a Christian, but just because the person doesn't want to have something put in their hand at that moment. So don't take rejection to heart, like I do. Just learn from the child who is taking his first steps. If he falls over and bruises himself, he doesn't give up. He gets up again, and that's how we learn to walk and to mature as human beings.

DIGGING DEEPER

1. The world often thinks they have the smile of a kind, gentle God of love. What do the following verses tell us about man's true standing with God?

John 3:36

Romans 2:5,6

Colossians 1:21

2. Ecclesiastes 7:29 tells us, "God made man upright, but they have sought out many schemes." List some of the evidences of the Fall from the below verses:

1 Corinthians 6:9–11

Ephesians 2:1–3

Titus 3:3–5

3. In those same verses, note all that God did for us.

4. Based on the above information, why should we have compassion on this sinful world?

5. To help sinners understand the depth of God's love—to appreciate what He's done for them—we first have to convince them of the disease of sin. Look up the following verses and record what they say about the functions of God's moral Law in witnessing:

1 Timothy 1:8–11

Romans 2:15

Romans 3:19,20

Romans 7:7,13

Galatians 3:24

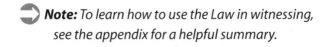 **Note:** *To learn how to use the Law in witnessing, see the appendix for a helpful summary.*

MEMORY VERSE

"For I am not ashamed of the gospel of Christ, for it is the power of God to salvation for everyone who believes…" —**Romans 1:16**

*To better understand the vital concept of biblical evangelism, please take time to listen to "Hell's Best Kept Secret," our most important message: **HellsBestKeptSecret.com***

THE NATURE OF GOD

OPEN IN PRAYER

SHARE YOUR EXPERIENCES

Briefly share the results of the previous session's "Sharing Made Simple" assignment. You were to leave ten gospel tracts somewhere, as well as be friendly and personally hand at least one tract to a stranger. Were you fearful before you did it? How did it go?

RAY // FOR YOUR REFLECTION

As Christians, we should be discerning. We should make sure that we don't spend our precious time watching and listening to things that really don't matter in the light of eternity.

We should rather put our time into studying the Scriptures—especially the character of God. All the fascinating, wonderful, and important doctrines of Scripture stand upon one foundation: the nature of our Creator. And if that foundation isn't firm, the building will topple. What you and I believe about God matters, because everything we think, say, and do will be governed by our understanding of who He is.

It is vital to keep in mind that human nature gravitates toward idolatry as a moth does to a flickering flame. Idolatry relieves us of the weight of guilt and opens the door to the delirious pleasures of sin. So we must do everything we can to guard our sinful hearts against making up an image of God that is not revealed in Scripture.

The way to guard against this is to crowd out the weeds with fruit-bearing plants. Leave no room for error by filling your mind with truths revealed in Scripture. Cram it full of Bible verses that paint a biblical picture of God as He is. He is holy. He is just. He will by no means clear the guilty. His morally perfect eyes follow every thought of every human heart, and His passion for justice hangs over every guilty sinner like a massive anvil, waiting to come down in wrath.

"But," says the Christian, "we have the cross, and that shows that God is rich in mercy, and that He loves us with an everlasting love." This is true. We have the strong consolation that, while we were sinners, Christ died for us. That is an eternal source of joy for the believer. The cross explodes gratitude in the heart of every sinner whose sin has been washed away by the shed blood of Jesus Christ.

However (and it's a huge "however"), we must never forget that the cross exists only because God is holy and just. And the knowledge of His uncompromising holiness (seen in that dreadful cross) will be a bulwark for us to keep evil out of our own hearts. The Scriptures say, "By the fear of the LORD one departs from evil" (Proverbs 16:6), and without the fear of the Lord we will embrace the hot coals of evil with both arms.

A right understanding of what happened on the cross—that we were redeemed not with corruptible things, but with the precious blood of Christ—will cause us to tremble and stay far away from sin. And that will be to our eternal salvation. There is nothing more important.

DISCUSSION QUESTIONS

1. Explain what a worldview is. How does our worldview affect the way we live?

2. What is "naturalism," and how does that govern a person's beliefs?

3. What are some areas where the Christian and the naturalistic worldviews clash?

4. What do the ungodly do to the truth, according to Romans chapter 1? Have you ever seen this happen?

5. If someone sincerely asks how we know God exists, we should answer them. But if a skeptic is mocking and hostile, what should we talk to them about and why?

6. How would you answer the question, "Who made God?"

The universe is not eternal

According to scientist Stephen Hawking, "All the evidence seems to indicate that the universe has not existed forever...Rather, the universe, and time itself, had a beginning in the Big Bang." He explains, "In fact, the theory that the universe has existed forever is in serious difficulty with the Second Law of Thermodynamics. The Second Law states that disorder always increases with time. Like the argument about human progress, it indicates that there must have been a beginning. Otherwise, the universe would be in a state of complete disorder by now, and everything would be at the same temperature" (Public Lecture, "The Beginning of Time").

7. What is often the motive behind skeptics attacking God's character?

8. Why is context so important when interpreting Scripture? Give some examples of verses that skeptics have taken out of context.

9. How could you respond if someone asked, "How can a loving God send someone to Hell?"

QUOTE // UNQUOTE

"We must earnestly endeavor to know the truth of the biblical worldview and to make it known with integrity to as many people as possible with the best arguments available. To know God in Christ means that we desire to make Christian truth available to others in the most compelling form possible. To be created in God's rational, moral and relational image means that our entire being should be aimed at the glorification of God in Christian witness. A significant part of that witness is Christian apologetics."

—**Douglas Groothuis**

A READY ANSWER

God will not "torture" anyone. He will simply give them justice. A criminal who viciously raped three teenage girls may believe that his being thrown into a cold prison cell is torture. The judge knows better. He calls it justice.

God will damn rebellious sinners from all that is good in a prison called "Hell." He gave them life and lavished His goodness upon them, and they despised Him, violated His Law, and then refused His mercy. He is extremely kind and "rich" in mercy, and offers complete forgiveness to all who repent and obey the gospel. Those who despise that mercy will get what the Bible calls "equity." Equity, according to the dictionary, is "the quality of being fair or impartial; fairness; impartiality: the equity of Solomon." In law, it is "the application of the dictates of conscience or the principles of natural justice to the settlement of controversies." In other words, impartially doing what is right, fair, and just.

The Bible tells us that God takes no pleasure in the death of the wicked (Ezekiel 33:11). His Word even says that "mercy triumphs over judgment" (James 2:13), meaning that God would rather see someone sorrowful and repentant and have their sins forgiven, than receive the full wrath of His justice. But if sinners remain hard and impenitent, His Word warns, "But in accordance with your hardness and your impenitent heart you are treasuring up for yourself wrath in the day of wrath and revelation of the righteous judgment of God, who 'will render to each one according to his deeds'" (Romans 2:5,6).

C. S. Lewis said, "Sin is man's saying to God throughout life, 'Go away and leave me alone.' Hell is God's finally saying to man, 'You may have your wish.' It is God's leaving man to himself, as man has chosen."

(Excerpted from *The Evidence Bible*.)

SHARING MADE SIMPLE

🌀 *Group Leader: Provide enough tracts to give each person ten.*

Pride is so subtle. It can stop us from giving out gospel tracts. We are concerned about what people think of us. We call it shyness, or embarrassment, or an inferiority complex. Anything but what it is: we are proud.

The Bible says that Jesus humbled Himself to the point of death, enduring the humiliation of the cross, so that you and I could have everlasting life. He humbled Himself, "despising the shame" (Hebrews 12:2).

God isn't asking us to be nailed to a physical cross. He's not asking us to hang in agony with pierced hands and feet. But He is wanting to use our crucified hands and feet for His purposes. And that's what happens when we share the gospel with an unbeliever—someone who is going to be damned in Hell if he dies in his sins.

So lift up your head and boldly say, "I am not ashamed of the gospel of Christ, for it is the power of God to salvation for everyone who believes..." (Romans 1:16).

With those thoughts in mind, your assignment this week is to break the sound barrier. You are going to actually talk to another human being about the things that really matter. So far you have given out tracts, planting seeds of the gospel. That's wonderful. Now you are going to follow up by simply saying, "It's a gospel tract. Do you think there's an afterlife? What do you think happens after somebody dies?"

Whatever answer he gives, follow up with another question. If he says, "No," ask him why he believes that. If he says, "Yes," ask him if he thinks he's good enough to make it to Heaven. Then take him through the Ten Commandments to bring the knowledge of sin.

🌀 *Note: If you need help, see the appendix for tips on how to do this biblically.*

DIGGING DEEPER

1. We know every painting must have a painter; everything that's made must have a maker. "For every house is built by someone, but He who built all things is God" (Hebrews 3:4). God alone has no beginning and exists outside the dimension of time. Note what these verses say about this aspect of God's nature:

   Psalm 90:2

   1 Timothy 1:17

   Titus 1:2

2. The world may use phrases such as "sure as Hell," but they don't have a biblical understanding of Hell. For those who are expecting a party place, how can you use the following verses to explain what it's really like?

   Matthew 13:41,42

Mark 9:47,48

Jude 7

Revelation 20:10

3. The lost often picture a God who is too kind and gentle to send any-one to Hell. Yet He is also a God of righteousness, holiness, and judgment. What can we learn about God as Judge in the following verses?

Psalm 7:11

Psalm 98:9

Numbers 14:18

Ecclesiastes 12:14

4. Read 2 Corinthians 5:10,11 and Acts 10:42. Given the reality of a holy God and an eternal Hell, what are we to do in response?

MEMORY VERSE

"The LORD is righteous in all His ways, gracious in all His works. The LORD is near to all who call upon Him, to all who call upon Him in truth." —**Psalm 145:17,18**

CHARACTER ASSASSINATION

OPEN IN PRAYER

SHARE YOUR EXPERIENCES

Briefly share the results of the previous session's "Sharing Made Simple" assignment. As you continued handing out tracts, this time you were to start a conversation with a stranger and take the person through the Commandments. How did the person respond? Is there anything you wish you had done differently?

RAY // FOR YOUR REFLECTION

Proverbs 6:17 says that God hates "a proud look." That look is esteemed by the world—whether it is the look of a gay pride march, or the peacocks that strut down the walk, modeling in a fashion parade. For the godly, there is something repulsive about someone who boasts that they are the greatest and how no one can beat them at their game.

As we grow in godliness and appreciate the virtues of God's character so displayed in the Savior, the ways of this world become nauseating. It becomes easy to see that the things highly esteemed among men are an abomination in the eyes of God. The secular world also boasts in every area. It boasts of discoveries of bogus science, it boasts of the achievements of Hollywood, and the most evil of people are upheld as heroes. Yet they are blasphemers, adulterers, homosexuals, fornicators, killers of babies in the womb, lovers of violence, lovers of money, and their films are nothing but a vehicle to promote their godless standards.

Jesus' description of human nature is so applicable:

"For from within, out of the heart of men, proceed evil thoughts, adulteries, fornications, murders, thefts, covetousness, wickedness, deceit, lewdness, an evil eye, blasphemy, pride, foolishness. All these evil things come from within and defile a man." (Mark 7:20–23)

These sinful men love the darkness and hate the light, and it's their pride that keeps them away from the light of the kingdom of God: "The wicked in his proud countenance does not seek God; God is in none of his thoughts" (Psalm 10:4). How these lost people need the gospel! They influence generations for evil and not for good. Such is the way of pride.

But in a world that esteems the proud look, humility is like a glorious breath of fresh air. Your humility, especially as you encounter contentious people, will make your words that much more impactful.

VIEW THE VIDEO // Character Assassination (26 minutes)

DISCUSSION QUESTIONS

1. Have you ever been mocked for your faith? How did you react?

2. Why do you think we are blessed when we suffer persecution?

3. How should a Christian define "success"?

4. How do you feel when you see a Christian being argumentative while sharing the gospel? Explain 2 Timothy 2:23–25.

5. What is the most loving thing you can do for an unsaved person?

6. Name some keys to walking in humility. What puffs us up with pride?

7. In witnessing, what does it mean to not "cast your pearls before swine" (Matthew 7:6)? How does that affect our message?

8. Has Christianity caused most wars in history? Explain.

9. When someone claims that Christians don't believe in science, how could you respond?

10. When people say that society determines what is right, how can you help them see the inconsistencies in their thinking?

" Ultimately, apologetics points people to our hope, Jesus Himself. That's why 'we demolish arguments and every high-minded thing that is raised up against the knowledge of God, taking every thought captive to the obedience of Christ' (2 Corinthians 10:4,5). Objections raised against Jesus must be demolished. But notice something. The Bible doesn't say we demolish people. Rather we demolish arguments. Belittling others is not our goal. Merely winning arguments is not enough. Instead, we remove obstacles of doubt to Christianity so people can take a serious look at Christ, the only source of hope for this world. True apologetics is hopeful. "

—Brett Kunkle

A READY ANSWER

Relativism

By Mark Spence

Relativism is the philosophical position that all points of view are equally valid, and that all truth is left up to the individual to define. This means that all moral positions, all religious systems, all political movements are truths that are relative to the individual. In other words, there are no right or wrong answers... to anything!

It's easy to recognize relativism because most of its statements sound intellectual but they are simply ridiculous and self-refuting. They go something like this:

"You can't know anything for sure."

"You shouldn't judge."

"Nobody's right."

"You can't know anything."

"What is true for you is not true for me."

The easiest way to refute statements like these is to simply turn them back around.

- "You can't know anything for *sure*."

  Are you *sure* of that? Are you *sure* you can't know anything for *sure*?

- "You shouldn't *judge*."

  Is that your *judgment*? And if you shouldn't *judge*, then why are you *judging* my *judgment*?

- "*Nobody's* right."

  Are you *right*? Are you right that *nobody's* right? And if you are *right*, then you're *wrong* about *nobody* being right.

- "You can't *know* anything."

  Do you *know* that? Do you *know* that you can't *know* anything?

- "What is *true* for you is not *true* for me."

  Well, that's *true*. And what is *true* for me is that you are wrong.

So, the next time you're confronted with that relativity nonsense, just turn it around to question the person's logic and help him realize that his point of view is just plain silly.

(Excerpted from *The Evidence Bible*.)

SHARING MADE SIMPLE

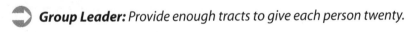 **Group Leader:** *Provide enough tracts to give each person twenty.*

Would you consider yourself to be a thick-skinned person? To be thick-skinned means to be "insensitive to criticism or insults." The way to measure the thickness of your skin is to consider how you deal with criticism. Let's say you have a great idea and you send it to a friend. You can't wait to hear him praise you for your initiative. Instead, he thinks it's a dumb idea. He even says it is a waste of time and money. How do you react? Are you mad at him, or glad that you have a friend who cares enough to speak the truth?

The biblical word for being thick-skinned is "grace." If you have grace, you will hardly notice when others tread on your toes. You will instead try to justify them, rather than feel sorry for yourself. Grace will protect you against having a bitter spirit; it will make you happier and healthier as a Christian.

And so arm yourself with grace as you speak to people. In Colossians 4:6, grace is likened to salt: "Let your speech always be with grace, seasoned with salt, that you may know how you ought to answer each one." Salt gives food a good taste. Everything we say should be in good taste.

This week, determine to go somewhere crowded and give out twenty tracts. As before, use the tracts as ice-breakers to start conversations, with the goal of talking with at least two people about the gospel. Just hand someone a tract, and as they take it you are to ask a warm and genuine, "How are you?" If they answer warmly, take that as an invitation to ask for their name and tell them yours. Like this: "Did you get one of these? My name is ____. That's a gospel tract. Do you think there's an afterlife?" Then repeat what you did previously.

As you do so, pray that your words would always be gracious. This is not a one-time exercise. This is going to become a way of life, where you live for others and think with an eternal perspective.

DIGGING DEEPER

1. In the book of Acts, you'll find that it didn't take long for persecution to begin against the church (starting in chapter 4), and that in all but five chapters the believers faced severe hardships and even death for their faith. Record what the following verses tell us about persecution and how we are to respond.

Matthew 5:11,12

1 Peter 1:6,7

1 Peter 4:12–14

James 1:2–4

2. What do the above verses say about the benefits of persecution?

3. In the following verses, identify the attitudes we are to have. Which are you currently applying in your evangelistic witness?

Matthew 5:43–45

Philippians 2:3,4

2 Timothy 2:24–26

1 Peter 3:8,9

4. What does the Bible say about professed Christians who are hateful toward homosexuals or others? (See 1 Corinthians 13:1–3 and 1 John 4:20,21.) What should be our attitude toward homosexuals?

MEMORY VERSE

"Therefore, as the elect of God, holy and beloved, put on tender mercies, kindness, humility, meekness, longsuffering; bearing with one another, and forgiving one another, if anyone has a complaint against another; even as Christ forgave you, so you also must do." —**Colossians 3:12,13**

THE BIBLE

OPEN IN PRAYER

SHARE YOUR EXPERIENCES

Briefly share the results of the previous session's "Sharing Made Simple" assignment. As you continued handing out tracts, were you able to get into one or more witnessing conversations? How did they go? Did you encounter any questions you weren't (yet) able to answer? If so, you now know which questions to research so you're ready for the next time.

RAY // FOR YOUR REFLECTION

As the world has become darker with its normalization of sin, it has shown an increasing contempt for God's Word. Pseudo-science is used to explain human origins, while the Bible is touted as being anti-science. Yet Darwinian evolution has no scientific basis; it is neither proven nor provable and has to be accepted by blind faith.

Perhaps more than ever before in history we need to realize that the Bible's creation account stands the scientific test, and we need to know how to credibly defend the faith against its many adversaries and mockers. How well do you know the Bible?

Keep in mind the Scriptures are made up of sixty-six different books, written over a period of about 1,500 years by about forty authors—some of whom were fishermen, tax collectors, prophets, and kings—and yet they have one common theme running through them.

The Bible is the divinely inspired, unique revelation of God's nature and His character. Its message is seen in His promise to free man from his greatest enemy, death. The Old Testament contains the promise, and the New Testament tells us the fulfillment.

This revelation of His will is condensed in the world's most hated and reviled Book. Yet it's also the most popular and beloved Book because it shows the godly that in the midst of a world of injustice, there is One who loves what is right and good and will hold evil men accountable. It is loved because we see the fulfillment of God's promised plan—His great love for sinners—so evidently demonstrated on the cross of Calvary.

The holy Scriptures are an oasis in the desert, a lighthouse in the greatest of all storms. They are an ever-present and inexhaustible comfort in life's many trials.

The Bible is more than a defensive wall against the pains of life. It is an attacking weapon against the enemy of our souls. The Word of God is living and powerful, a sharp two-edged sword that cuts to the hearts of demons and of sinful men and women. Jesus quoted the words of Scripture during His time of temptation in the desert and sent the devil running. We need to learn to do the same.

But the Bible is even more than a tonic for the weary soul, and the weapon of choice for the soldier of Christ. It is the official Instruction Book, given by the Maker for every area of life. It tells us the future before it comes to pass, so that we can know God is in control. That gives us great peace. It speaks of hope for the future—a hope that isn't confined to this short life. It reaches into eternity. Death becomes a beginning rather than an end. That gives us great joy.

The Scriptures also tell us how to be successful in human relationships, in marriage, in finances, in prayer, in sexuality, in child rearing, in how to effectively reach the lost, and a thousand other issues. If only the world would listen to its wonderful wisdom, it would save itself so much pain, both in this life and in the life to come.

Read the Bible daily, search out its treasures of truth, and live by its words. Quote it to the enemy, take comfort in its precious promises, and let its words motivate you to reach out to those who are seated in the shadow of death.

VIEW THE VIDEO // The Bible (24 minutes)

DISCUSSION QUESTIONS

1. How would you answer the claim that the Bible is full of mistakes?

2. What is the key to learning Scripture?

3. How could you respond when people say the Bible isn't trustworthy because it was "written by men"?

4. What does it mean that the Bible was "inspired" by God?

5. When someone makes opposing statements, why is it important to ask where they get their information?

6. How do the godly approach a seeming contradiction in the Bible?

7. Explain why unbelievers hate the Bible.

8. Why are Christians to contend for the faith—what is our agenda?

9. How would you explain the thread of continuity that runs through the Bible?

10. In what ways is the atheist like the prodigal son (Luke 15)?

QUOTE // UNQUOTE

"We need to help people be aware of the important issues with which they will need to contend. In the area of apologetics, we must give reasons for why we believe. We see so many believers who have only a superficial understanding of Scripture and have no basis for saying why the Christian faith is true and or why he is not a Hindu or a Muslim. Without that awareness of an objective foundation for belief, they will buy into books like *The Da Vinci Code* and will be much more vulnerable to the tactics of religious movements like Mormonism or Jehovah's Witnesses. Because they are not biblically or theologically founded, they can become more easily confused and rattled when they read a book like Richard Dawkins's *The God Delusion*. They just have not thought deeply about their own faith; so they become swayed by anti- or non-Christian perspectives."

—Paul Copan

A READY ANSWER

Contradictions in the Bible—Why Are They There?

The Bible has many *seeming* contradictions within its pages. For example, the four Gospels give four differing accounts as to what was written on the sign that hung on the cross. Matthew said, "This is Jesus the King of the Jews" (27:37). However, Mark contradicts that with "The King of the Jews" (15:26). Luke says something different:

"This is the King of the Jews" (23:38), and John maintains that the sign said "Jesus of Nazareth, the King of the Jews" (19:19). Those who are *looking* for contradictions may therefore say, "See—the Bible is full of mistakes!" and choose to reject it entirely as being untrustworthy. However, those who trust God have no problem harmonizing the Gospels. There is no contradiction if the sign simply said, "This is Jesus of Nazareth, the King of the Jews."

The godly base their confidence on two truths: 1) "all Scripture is given by inspiration of God" (2 Timothy 3:16); and 2) an elementary rule of Scripture is that God has deliberately included *seeming* contradictions in His Word to "snare" the proud. He has "hidden" things from the "wise and prudent" and "revealed them to babes" (Luke 10:21), purposely choosing foolish things to confound the wise (1 Corinthians 1:27). If an ungodly man refuses to humble himself and obey the gospel, and instead desires to build a case against the Bible, God gives him enough material to build his own gallows.

This incredible principle is clearly illustrated in the account of the capture of Zedekiah, king of Judah. Jeremiah the prophet told Zedekiah that God would judge him. He was informed that he would be "delivered into his hand; your eyes shall see the eyes of the king of Babylon, he shall speak with you face to face, and you shall go to Babylon" (Jeremiah 34:3). This is confirmed in Jeremiah 39:5–7 where we are told that he was captured and brought to King Nebuchadnezzar, then they "bound him with bronze fetters to carry him off to Babylon." However, in Ezekiel 12:13, God warned, "I will bring him to Babylon …*yet he shall not see it*, though he shall die there" (emphasis added).

Here is material to build a case against the Bible! It is an obvious mistake. Three Bible verses say that the king would go to Babylon, and yet the Bible in another place says that he would not see Babylon. How can someone be taken somewhere and not see it? It makes no sense at all—unless Zedekiah was blinded. And that is precisely what happened. Zedekiah saw Nebuchadnezzar face to face, saw his sons killed before his eyes, then "the king of Babylon…put out Zedekiah's eyes" before taking him to Babylon (Jeremiah 39:6,7).

This is the underlying principle behind the many "contradictions" of Holy Scripture (such as how many horses David had, who was the first to arrive at the tomb after the resurrection of Jesus, etc.). God has turned the tables on proud, arrogant, self-righteous man. When man proudly stands outside of the kingdom of God, and seeks to justify his sinfulness through evidence he thinks discredits the Bible, he doesn't realize that God has simply lowered the door of life, so that only those willing to exercise childlike faith and bow in humility may enter.

It is interesting to note that the seeming contradictions in the four Gospels attest to the fact that there was no corroboration between the writers.

(Excerpted from *The Evidence Bible.*)

SHARING MADE SIMPLE

 Group Leader: *Provide enough tracts to give each person twenty.*

This week's assignment is to give out twenty tracts in a crowded place, but this time initiate at least four conversations. Stretch yourself. Run at Goliath. Don't let fear come near you. This is too important for such trivialities.

As an interesting twist, you may want to ask people who wrote the Bible. You may be surprised at the answers you receive, but be prepared to gently inform them of its true Author. Whatever you do, be sure to take them through the Commandments into the good news of the cross.

Though this is our last step in learning how to share the message of everlasting life, let it become an ongoing, lifelong marathon—as you run with endurance the race that is set before you: "to testify to the gospel of the grace of God" (Hebrews 12:1; Acts 20:24).

DIGGING DEEPER

1. If the Son of God believed the Scriptures, we should trust them too. Jesus referred to Genesis 1–11 in particular on six occasions. What are some biblical accounts that the world mocks as "fairy tales" that Jesus treated as literal historical events?

    Matthew 19:4,5

    Matthew 12:39,40

    Luke 17:26–32

2. As we contend for the faith, we need to remember we are in the midst of a spiritual battle and our enemy seeks to disarm us. In Ephesians 6:17 and Hebrews 4:12, what does Scripture say about our "weapon"?

3. Read Matthew 4:1–11. When facing temptation by Satan, what did Jesus use as "defense"? How was He able to do this?

4. So that we can reason with people from the Scriptures, as was Paul's custom (Acts 17:2), what does Scripture advise us to do with the Word of God?

Joshua 1:8

Psalm 119:11

Acts 17:11

James 1:22

5. Jesus said to "search" the Scriptures, so don't let a superficial reading of God's Word cheat you of amazing truths. List some of the many benefits of God's Word for mankind, according to the following verses:

Psalm 119:30,105

Romans 15:4

2 Timothy 3:15

2 Timothy 3:16,17

MEMORY VERSE

"Knowing this first, that no prophecy of Scripture is of any private interpretation, for prophecy never came by the will of man, but holy men of God spoke as they were moved by the Holy Spirit." —**2 Peter 1:20,21**

HOW TO WITNESS

I f you're not familiar with the use of the Law in evangelism, this appendix will summarize the "Way of the Master" biblical approach (from the "Way of the Master" Basic Training Course Study Guide). If you've gone through the training course, this information may serve as a handy refresher for you and includes some helpful points to remember when witnessing.

STARTING A WITNESSING ENCOUNTER

To get your feet wet in witnessing, an easy first step is learning to be friendly and talk with people. This may seem obvious, but make a habit of talking to your neighbors and coworkers regularly. Then practice being friendly with people at the park, at the gas station, or at the grocery store. Perhaps you already have an outgoing and friendly personality—that's great! If you tend to be a shy, introverted person, try to open up a little and start greeting people. A simple, "Hi, how are you?" isn't difficult. Or say, "Nice day, isn't it? My name is so and so…" With a bit of practice, anyone can learn to be friendly. Most people respond warmly to warmth.

To share our faith effectively, we must let people know that we are not "weirdos" or religious fanatics. We must show them that we care, and we start by being friendly. A good friend (who is admittedly quite shy) mentioned that he and a buddy went to the park on a Saturday afternoon, just to practice being friendly to strangers. They had a great time, and had so much fun that they couldn't wait to get out the following weekend to take the next step.

After you have gained a measure of confidence in speaking to strangers, you can swing to the subject of spiritual things.

It's not wise to walk up to people and immediately assault them with talk about Jesus. They'll most likely think you're strange. Instead, start in the natural realm (everyday things) and then swing to the spiritual realm. That's what Jesus did (see John chapter 4). He began talking with the woman at the well about natural things, then He swung to the spiritual. You may want to talk about sports or the weather, and then perhaps use something in the news to transition to the subject of spiritual things.

Or you can use a gospel tract as a conversational "ice-breaker." It doesn't matter how you do it, as long as you do it. Start in the natural realm so the person doesn't think you're a religious nut, and then make the transition any way you want. That will lead you directly into the conversation about God.

WDJD: THE FOUR STEPPINGSTONES

By following the WDJD outline, you can confidently lead any witnessing encounter. You will be in control of every conversation you have about your faith. Imagine—you will know exactly where you are in a conversation and you will know exactly where it is going. You don't have to study Greek or understand archaeology; you just have to follow the four "steppingstones" to reach your goal. You can say goodbye to your fears.

There is no doubt that the first point is the most difficult to ask. Once you've brought up the subject of spiritual things, it becomes much easier. Here are the four steppingstones in the WDJD acronym.

W: Would you consider yourself to be a good person?

You will be surprised to find that people are not offended by this question. If they say "No" (highly unlikely), ask them what they mean. Remember, you are asking people about their favorite subject —themselves. Most likely you'll find that they are kidding or that they've done something in their life that they feel badly about.

Otherwise, expect individuals to respond, "I'm a pretty good person," or, "I'm a *really* good person." This reveals their pride and their self-righteousness. At this point you are ready to use the Law (the Ten Commandments) to humble them . . . the way Jesus did. Now move to the next steppingstone.

D: Do you think you have kept the Ten Commandments?

Some will say yes, others will say no. Regardless, you simply continue by saying, "Let's take a look at a few and see. Have you ever told a lie?" Some will admit to lying; others will say they have told only "white lies"; a few will claim they have never lied even once. Gently press the issue: "Do you mean to say that you have never told anyone a lie to deceive them? Even once?" Usually they will say something like, "Maybe when I was a kid." Ask, "What does that make you?" They will hesitate to say, but get them to admit, "A liar."

People do not get angry with this approach; instead, they become sober. They may declare, "I don't believe in the Bible." Simply continue on your course. If they argue about the Bible, say, "I know you don't believe it. I am simply sharing with you what the Bible says. Okay? Let's keep going."

Continue going through the Commandments. You may want to ask about stealing next, then the Seventh Commandment, then the Third. Here is an example of how to go through each one:

#9   We covered "lying" above.

#8   "Have you ever stolen anything?" Many will claim that they haven't. "Have you ever taken anything that did not belong to you, regardless of its value—anything? Even when you were younger? Be honest before God." Some will try to trivialize theft by saying that they stole when they were a child. Ask, "What does that make you?" and press them to say, "A thief."

#7 "Have you ever committed adultery?" Again, most will say no. Add, "Jesus said, 'Whoever looks at a woman to lust for her has already committed adultery with her in his heart.' Have you ever looked at someone with lust?"

#3 "Have you ever taken the Lord's name in vain?" Some will try to wiggle out of this, but just press a little: "You mean you have never used God's name casually, or to express anger?" Most will admit to this one. Then gently explain, "So instead of using a four-letter filth word to express disgust, you have taken the name of the One who gave you life and everything that is precious to you, and you have dragged it through the mud. People don't even use Saddam Hussein's name to curse, and you have used Almighty God's name? That is called 'blasphemy,' and God promises that He will not hold anyone guiltless who takes His name in vain."

Note: You should be noticing something at this point. The individual will either grow quiet (his "mouth may be stopped" by the Law, Roman 3:19) or will be getting agitated. If the person seems to recognize his guilt, you may want to say at this point, "By your own admission, you're a lying thief, a blasphemer, and an adulterer at heart, and we've only looked at four of the Ten Commandments." If he is still trying to defend himself ("I'm not a bad person"), go through a few more Commandments.

#6 "Have you ever murdered anyone?" Obviously, most will say that they haven't. Point out, "Jesus said that if you merely call your brother a fool, you are in danger of judgment, and the Bible says if you've ever hated anyone, you are a murderer in God's eyes. God does not simply judge actions, He knows the intentions of the heart."

#1 "Have you always put God first in your life?" Most will admit that they haven't. "God says that He should be the primary love of our life. In fact, Jesus said that our love for God should be so great that our love for our parents, kids, friends, even our own lives should seem like hatred by comparison."

#2 "Have you ever made an idol, a god to suit yourself?" People will usually say that they haven't. "Have you pursued money more than God? Then you have made money an idol. Have you given work more attention than God? Then work is an idol. If you think, 'God is loving and wouldn't send me to Hell,' you are correct; your god wouldn't send anyone to Hell, because your god doesn't exist. He is a figment of your imagination. You've created a god in your own mind that you're more comfortable with, and that is called 'idolatry.' It's the oldest sin in the Book and God warns us that idolaters will not inherit the Kingdom of God."

#5 "Have you always honored your parents, treating them in a way that is pleasing to God?"

#10 "Have you ever coveted, or jealously desired something that did not belong to you? Covetousness reveals a lack of gratitude for what God has already given you."

#4 "Have you kept the Sabbath holy? God requires one day out of seven for you to rest and acknowledge Him, and you have failed to give Him what He has demanded. How many times have you neglected to bow your head before your meal and thank Him for the food He has provided? How many thousands of times do you think you've just greedily dug in without thanking your Provider?"

J—Judgment: If God judges you by the Ten Commandments on the Day of Judgment, will you be *innocent* or *guilty*?

If the individual has not yet begun to show signs of conviction, he will more than likely start now. Most people will sense where you are going with the conversation and say, "Innocent." But they must understand and confess their guilt if they are ever to come to Jesus (see Proverbs 28:13). The following will help them do that. Use this as a guide in directing the conversation and dealing with common responses. Again, this is not a script for what to say; feel free to use your own words.

Them: "I'm a pretty good person."

You: "You just told me that you broke God's Commandments, the moral Law. By your own admission, you're a lying thief, an adulterer at heart, a murderer, and a blasphemer. Think about it. Will you be innocent or guilty?"

Them: "But I haven't done those things for a long time."

You: "Imagine saying that in a court of law. 'Judge, I know I am guilty but it has been years.' He won't ignore your crime. He will see that justice is served and will punish you no matter how much time has elapsed. The courts punish war criminals from decades ago, and God doesn't forget sin no matter how long ago a person did it. Do you think you will be innocent or guilty?"

Them: "But I have done more good than bad."

You: "Again, think of a court of law. If you have broken the law, you are guilty. It doesn't matter how many good deeds you've done when you are being tried for your crime. You have broken God's Law. Will you be innocent or guilty?"

Them: "But that's man's law. God is different."

You: "You're right. God can never be bribed. And His standards are much higher than a human judge's. He loves justice and has promised that He will punish not only murderers and rapists, but also liars, thieves, adulterers, and blasphemers. You are in big trouble, aren't you?"

Often, people become awakened (aware of their sin), but not alarmed. In other words, they understand they have broken God's Law, but it seems that they just don't care. Your goal is to see them alarmed, because they should be—they are in great danger. This line of reasoning can help:

Let's imagine that a computer chip has been placed behind your ear, and it records everything that runs through your mind for a whole week: every secret thought, every deed, and every word that comes out of your mouth. Then all of your friends and family are called together and all of your thoughts are displayed on a big screen for them to see. How would that make you feel? Embarrassed? Ashamed? That is what will happen on the day when God requires you to give an account for everything you've said and done for your whole life. All of your secret thoughts will be laid before Him. You are in big trouble.

It's wonderful to get a confession of guilt, but if the person simply won't be honest and admit his guilt, at some point you may have to help him. Say, "If you would just be honest, you know you will be guilty before God. Besides, that is what the Bible says and if you claim to be innocent, you are calling God a liar."

D—Destiny: Will you go to Heaven or Hell?

Gently ask, "Do you think you will go to Heaven or Hell?" People won't be offended because you are simply asking a question, rather than telling them where they're going. Some will say, "Hell," but most will say, "Heaven." If they think they are going to Heaven, you can use this analogy:

Consider this. You are standing in a court of law, guilty of a serious crime. There is a $100,000 fine. The judge says, "You are guilty. Anything to say before I pass sentence?" You answer, "Yes, Judge. I'm sorry for what I have done. Please forgive me." Can a good judge let you go simply because you say that you are sorry, or that you won't do it again? Of course not. There is a $100,000 fine that must be paid. However, if someone pays the fine for you, can the judge then let you go? Yes; once the fine has been paid, your debt to the law has been satisfied and the judge can set you free.

In the same way, each of us is guilty before God, and He will not let us go simply because we say that we're sorry or that we won't do it again. Of course, we should be sorry, and we shouldn't do it again. However, the fine for our crime must still be paid.

If the person responds by saying that this is man's justice, and that God's ways are different, agree with him. Say that God's justice is far harsher than man's justice, and that His standards are infinitely higher.

Don't be afraid to tell people that if they die in their sins, the Bible makes it clear that they will go to Hell. Ask, "Does that concern you?"

If they say that it doesn't concern them, or if you sense they are not humbled and don't recognize their need of God's forgiveness, it's very helpful to describe what Hell is like until they show signs of concern. According to the Bible, Hell is a place of eternal, conscious torment, where "the worm dies not, and the fire is not quenched"; there is "weeping and gnashing of teeth," "everlasting punishment," "shame and everlasting contempt," and "eternal fire...the blackness of darkness for ever." Tell them that you don't want them to go to Hell, and God doesn't want them to go to Hell. Plead with them. If they do not seem concerned, it may be that they are just hiding it.

Don't feel pressured to give the Good News to a proud, self-righteous (rebellious, cussing, arrogant) sinner who is not willing to admit his guilt before God. Remember, Jesus didn't give the gospel to the rich, young ruler, because he needed the Law to humble him first. You will have to watch and listen carefully because humility is not always obvious.

If the person admits that it does concern him, only at that point should you go to the gospel. If you are able to detect humility (the person is no longer justifying and defending himself), or his responses indicate that he has been humbled, you now have the glorious pleasure of sharing the Good News.

SHARING THE GOSPEL

The Good News

Here's a good way to begin sharing the gospel: "God provided a way for you to be forgiven. The question is, how do you access this forgiveness?" Take the time to explain this thoroughly: "God loves you so much that He sent His only Son to suffer and die in your place, taking your punishment for you so that you could live. It's this simple: you broke the Law and Jesus paid your fine. Then Jesus rose from the dead and defeated death. If you will repent—turn away from sin—and place your trust in Jesus Christ alone as your Savior, God will forgive you and grant you everlasting life. He will change you from the inside out, and make you a new person in Christ."

This is the time to magnify the *love of God* to the sinner. Now you have the green light—go for it! Don't hold back: show the amazing length, width, depth, and height of God's love for the person as a sinner. This is when you pull out John 3:16. God offers complete forgiveness of sin and the gift of everlasting life *freely* to those who will surrender everything to Him through faith in Jesus Christ.

Ask the individual if he understands what you have told him. If he is willing to confess and turn from his sins and trust the Savior for his eternal salvation, encourage him to pray and ask God to forgive him.

The Prayer

Should we pray the traditional "sinner's prayer" with someone who we think is willing to turn from sin and trust in Christ? Perhaps this will shed some light on the subject: If someone you know committed adultery, would you lead him back to his wife and say, "Repeat after me: 'I am really sorry. I should not have slept with that woman'"? More than likely you wouldn't. She just wants to hear words of genuine repentance flow from his heart. It's the same with God.

If someone says he wants to pray right then and there, encourage him to do so. You might like to say, "You can pray right now. Confess your sins and turn from them, and then tell God you are placing your trust in Jesus as the Lord and Savior of your life. Surrender your heart to Him. After you've prayed, I'll pray for you."

Then make sure the person has a Bible (get him one if necessary), and encourage him to read it daily and obey what he reads. Also, encourage him to get into a Bible-believing, Christ-centered church.

If the person doesn't ask you to pray with him, let him go on his way, but encourage him to think deeply about your conversation and to get his heart right with the Lord as soon as possible. You can then leave him in the hands of a faithful God, who will continue to speak to him through His Holy Spirit and bring him to genuine repentance in His time.

RESOURCES

F or additional tips on evangelism and apologetics, please visit our website where you can sign up for our free weekly e-mail update. To learn how to share your faith the way Jesus did, don't miss these helpful resources:

Hell's Best Kept Secret / True and False Conversion: Listen to these vital messages free at HellsBestKeptSecret.com.

God Has a Wonderful Plan for Your Life: The Myth of the Modern Message: Our most important book (over 250,000 in print).

The Way of the Master Basic Training Course: This eight-week DVD course (based on the award-winning TV show) is our premier training tool for learning to share your faith biblically.

The Way of the Master Intermediate Training Course: This follow-up eight-week DVD course will help you witness to atheists, evolutionists, homosexuals, family members, false converts, and more.

School of Biblical Evangelism: Join more than 18,000 students worldwide—learn to witness and defend the faith in 101 online lessons. Also available in book form.

World Religions in a Nutshell: Learn the basic beliefs of other religions as well as how to witness to those in other faiths.

What *Did* Jesus Do? Examine the way that Jesus, the disciples, and great evangelists of the past reached the lost.

For a complete list of resources by Ray Comfort, visit **LivingWaters.com**, call 800-437-1893, or write to: Living Waters Publications, P.O. Box 1172, Bellflower, CA 90706.

THE
EVIDENCE BIBLE

"An invaluable tool for becoming a more effective witness." —FRANKLIN GRAHAM

The Evidence Bible (NKJV) arms you not just with apologetic information to refute the arguments of skeptics, but with practical evangelism training on how to lead them to Christ.

- Discover answers to over 200 questions such as: Why is there suffering? How could a loving God send people to hell? What about those who never hear of Jesus?

- In addition to thousands of verse-related comments, over 130 informative articles will enable you to better comprehend and communicate the Christian faith.

- Over two dozen articles on evolution will thoroughly prepare you to refute the theory.

- Dozens of articles on other religions will help you understand and address the beliefs of Mormons, Hindus, Muslims, Jehovah's Witnesses, cults, and others.

- Hundreds of inspiring quotes from renowned Christian leaders and practical tips on defending your faith will greatly encourage and equip you.

The Evidence Bible provides powerful and compelling evidence that will enrich your trust in God and His Word, deepen your love for the truth, and enable you to reach those you care about with the message of eternal life.

*Commended by Norman Geisler, Josh McDowell,
D. James Kennedy, Woodrow Kroll, Tim LaHaye,
Ken Ham, and many other Christian leaders.*